The
SWAN

...with the
ICEBERG LEGS...

*10 simple checks to make sure
you calmly stand out.*

Edward Mason

DISCLAIMER

This book is intended as a swift summary of some key principles in building a successful business. It is not intended to be a 'workshop manual' and it should not be used without involving the author whose experience can help interpret how best to apply the principles to any specific situation...

The author cannot be held responsible for the unauthorised use or interpretation of any of the contents.

Table
Of Contents

Churchill, if he'd had more time…

'I'D HAVE MADE IT SHORTER IF I'D HAD MORE TIME'

Whether it was Churchill or Wilde whose wit brought this line into our consciousness doesn't matter. The point is, I have had enough time to make this short. A career of more than 30 years in fact, including:

- a classical sales training with Rank Hovis MacDougall in the Co-ops and Cash & Carries of North-East England*

- being joint CEO of Claydon Heeley Jones Mason, a rapid-growth ad agency that we sold to the global market leader Omnicom. Much of the success of the agency was fuelled by a unique, strategic approach to pitching effectively

- 20+ subsequent years working with a fascinating range of organisations and leaders from long-established global brands such as Fortnum & Mason (no relation) and Cushman & Wakefield through to start-ups like the awesome Modern Baker SUPERLOAF, non-for-profits like The Welsh Football Association, and major Landed Estates on clarifying their differentiated proposition and how to communicate it

- co-founding True Royalty TV, the global Royal streaming service, and pitching to raise more than $18m to grow the business. I am still active in this business, and work with many others on honing their strategy and what differentiates them so that their communication becomes more effective.

If I sound rather un-English listing these out, forgive me: it's important for you to know that what I'm writing is thought-through enough to mean it can be brief, and that it works in practice.

Why so short? There are so many business books, many of which are good, some of which are inspiring even, but none of us has time to read them all. Most of them say what they need to say in the first chapter anyway...

It was the CEO of one client company who suggested the book should lead with the charts I use most often: he observed that what really helps is to have a simple frame of reference to guide leaders and companies through what appear to be complex situations.

Incidentally, you might think this book is written back to front. Why does a book whose thrust is about communication have eight chapters that have nothing apparently to do with pitching? The answer is in the title, a mash-up of firstly the good old iceberg analogy - where the beautiful piece you see above the water cannot exist without the hefty 90% beneath the surface that you never see – and then the cliched swan looking serene whilst paddling furiously under the water. If you want to communicate confidently, you've got to have tamed this challenging, sometimes contradictory and yet buoyant platform first.

Most of my work is helping people get the message right through **strategy** and then **differentiation**; the **presentation** part is the clichéd swan gracefully paddling along. Beneath the surface, there are more than just a couple of little legs to control whilst paddling furiously: more like two huge unwieldy icebergs which are trying to evade control. It takes determination, commitment, and concentration.

• • ● • •

*Like most difficult experiences, this sales rep training was invaluable in learning that things don't always run smoothly, however much prep you do.

Monday morning, Asda at Rawtenstall in the Peak District.

Store and warehouse check done by 9am, ready for appointment with the un-reconstructed old-school manager.

45 minutes of standing outside his office later:

"COME IN."
"Good morning, I'm the new rep from RHM…"
"F**k off."
"Erm, I've done the store-chec…"
"I said f**k off. Now F**K OFF."

Exit, pursued by barely any remaining dignity.

WHAT THIS
BOOK IS FOR...

Throughout this book I use the word 'pitch' to include a company 'Town Hall', a results presentation, a pitch to a potential investor, an interview (whichever side of it you are on...) and of course the classic bid for a major contract.

In each case, the 'pitch' is where you want – and need – to show yourself or your organisation at its best.

The worst thing you can do is to present an amazing story which you can't deliver on. If you try, you will probably get called out and lose the audience, wasting everyone's time and lowering morale in your team or organisation.

Most of the time, when I'm coaching people to pitch their organisation the biggest challenge is that they aren't *really* clear on what makes the organisation better than their rivals. So often, people will list out a number of attributes which are all important...but the same as their competition would cite.

Much of this book is about how to create or hone a strategy and communicate differentiation, building a team or even a whole organisation that stands up to scrutiny in the arena of pitching – and critically, actually delivering in action longer-term.

It's all based on my own experience throughout my career which is why it is peppered with examples to illustrate the points, as well as principles that I have learned from others.

There is a saying 'Nothing kills a bad product faster than good advertising'. The same principle applies to pitching…if you are building people's expectations to be greater than you can deliver, you need to be thinking about how you change the organisation.

That's what this book is for. There are ten checks in it. If you read each with an open mind you will find which ones you need to do something about. It's unlikely to be more than the nuancing of each that you need. But the difference between winning and losing a pitch, or capturing the hearts and minds of a team, or recruiting that rising star…or even being the star yourself: it's almost always a very marginal call.

EXECUTIVE SUMMARY

'Tell them what you're going to tell them. Tell them. Then tell them what you've told them." I've often thought there should be a National Cliché Day for us to reflect on these almost invisible sayings and re-appraise them: there is a reason they became so over-used and this one is no exception.

This is the narrative the 10 sections take into a little more depth:

1. It may seem tiresome, but change is ironically a constant in success. Once we accept that we can embrace the opportunities it opens up.

2. Very often, the things that need changing are the most entrenched 'truths'. These are not necessarily wrong but are frequently framed in the rear view mirror.

3. Addressing those and building a truly exciting vision for the road ahead can liberate the potential of people, teams and organisation.

4. That vision needs to be real to work – not just lip-service.

5. And it needs to be consistent in both how it is delivered and how it is communicated.

6. Only a proper team will make this all work – people understand that if the team does well, they do well themselves.

7. Working out who you, individually and as an organisation, are going to work best with is essential - as customers and as collaborators.

8. Proper insight into what's on their minds will unlock how best to communicate with them.

9. Distilling everything down to a compelling proposition takes a lot of hard work – it rarely happens effectively without it.

10. It's only once you master all this that you can reasonably expect to communicate effectively...

– but once you do, it's a super-power...

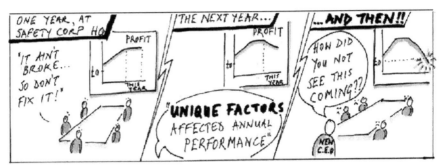

1:
IS IT SAFE TO
PLAY IT SAFE?

'If it ain't broke, don't fix it.' The most dangerous philosophy of them all, sanctioning lazy thought and inaction, and yet beguiling and all too commonly used.

Most of us recognise that it's worth the hassle of upgrading our phone from time to time, even if it is still working fine – the world has moved on. Why would we let our business gradually degrade just because it isn't technically broken? In relation to the competition, businesses in effect go backwards when they are not going forwards: there are always others evolving and innovating even when you're not, and they want to eat your lunch.

We have a tendency to cling to the status quo, because it's difficult to change. It means upheaval, coming out of one's comfort zone. Human nature – for most people – is to keep things the same…even when things are not that great as they are.

This is particularly true for a tranche of management that exists in many organisations – people who have a high-status role but who are quietly hoping to make it to the end of their career without the upheaval (and threat) of having to embrace the change they know is on the horizon.

However. 'It's not the strongest, or the most intelligent of a species that survive: it's the ones most ready to adapt.' Darwin to the rescue. It may be hard, but it is essential to be able to change.

The French have a saying: reculer pour mieux sauter. It doesn't sound so good in English, but it does make sense: 'to draw back in order to make a better jump'.

Every business leader needs to draw back in order to make a better jump. They need to do it every day, not just in developing grand strategic plans, just as a sports coach might teach a new technique - but only as part of a long-term plan for success. 'To fail to plan is to plan to fail' as the management cliché goes; but we should never forget John Lennon's pithy observation that 'life is what happens while you're making plans'.

The skill in this is in changing of your own volition: whilst things are going well.

At Fortnum's, we had to rebuild almost everything because not enough had changed over the previous 15 years. We had to create an 'accelerated evolution' - a huge upheaval that took three years and major investment – but it turned the previous growing losses into sustainable profit and more importantly, a reinvigorated sense of purpose and team that is still recognisable many years later.

At Claydon Heeley, the ad agency where I was joint CEO, we were constantly and deliberately drawing back: at every company meeting, every four months, we'd stand up in front of the whole team and explain how well the company was doing: and then, to an ironic groan, announce the changes we were going to make.

We were the ones in our market most ready to adapt: and we did more than survive, selling to Omnicom on a strong multiple, with other leading global advertising groups also bidding. Many of the 'alumni' of that business have gone on to other great successes, usually underpinned by the same philosophy of challenging conventional thinking.

The classic S-Curve appears in management theory in the writings of numerous experts. The remarkably astute Charles Handy is one who talks about the need to think not of just one S-Curve but of a whole series of them, some long, some short: but all of them deliberate. His point, eloquently made as ever, is that leadership has to be constantly vigilant, open-minded, flexible, and vigorous.

Get into the habit, and it is like a series of escalators going higher and higher.

Avoid it, and you'll see your competition glide by on the escalators as you stand and watch.

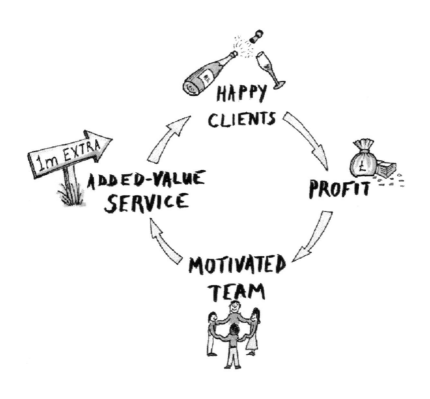

The service/profit chain:

If you overlook any one link, it all falls apart

2:

HAVE WE GOT OUR PRIORITIES RIGHT?

Working with the management board of a major international airline, it became very clear that the over-riding mentality of this huge organisation was that of an engineering firm - as it had been from the start. They put aeroplanes into the sky and people could use them to get around the world - safely. Under-standably, and rather reassuringly, engineers were held in very high esteem and what they said, went.

Customers, meanwhile, had learned that with some of the newer airlines they could have safe travel AND amazing ser-vice - and this choice was attracting strong custom.

For my client company, Customer Service, Marketing, HR and even Finance were all slightly regarded as nice-to-haves, with only Finance having even a remotely comparable status to Engineering. The two departments took it in turns to be in the ascendency, frustrating members of the team who could see the problems this caused and the opportunities being missed.

The breakthrough in redressing this imbalance was an exercise in freeing the team up from the pressures of everyday airline management. We challenged them to think what they would do if they were starting a *new* airline with both the ambition and the backing to be the world's favourite airline.

Using the Service-profit chain that is taught so effectively on the Harvard-based Omnicom Senior Management Programme, it soon became clear that sustainable profit would be dependent upon loyal and satisfied customers...and that they in turn would need not just the reassurance that the planes would stay in the air and run on time but also that flying would be an enjoyable experience: in other words, they wanted service...and that only comes from people who are motivated, who enjoy their work and are loyal to their employer. That, in turn, means that they would need not just to be remunerated well but looked after, well-trained, and enabled to enjoy what they do...and in turn that needs both great management and, of course, finance...

The same is true of pretty much any organisation, although we should always be wary of thinking that motivation is purely about money: it rarely is, even in organisations that are not especially purpose driven.

Incidentally, it is easy to assume as well that people in charities are especially driven by the purpose. My experience is that the bigger the charity, the more likely you are to meet people in management who are slightly snow-blind about the purpose and have become fiercely competitive for their team.

The Service-Profit Chain is very often the ideal way to refocus a team on what really matters.

'Not everything that can be measured counts, and not everything that counts can be measured' Albert Einstein.

"First you gotta find
out who you are.
Then you gotta do it,
on purpose."

3:
WHAT'S THE POINT
OF IT ALL?

Here's a cheating 'diagram': it's just words.

The quotation is Dolly Parton, explaining how to be success-ful.
It applies as much to businesses as it does to individuals.
I haven't found a better way of describing the core driver of success.

Here's what is happening around most meeting room tables:

Every successful organisation had a real purpose when it started: something in the mind of the founder or founders, the reason for launching it in the first place. Sometimes it's opportunity, sometimes necessity. In the case of successful businesses, it's usually the belief that we can do something better than other people. Enzo Ferrari believed he could build a better sports car than previously existed...Jo Malone saw a more engaging way to approach the scent market...pick any well-known business and there will be something in its make-up that drove its success in the beginning.

Now look at a business you know well and consider how clear its purpose is. And then consider whether everyone in that company would say the same thing.

If the organisation you're thinking about is where you are in a leadership role, you will* have a clear picture of where the business wants or needs to be in three to five years' time. Would your fellow leaders describe the same picture?

In most companies, it's like a Venn Diagram: some common ground but with an awful lot of blurring around the edges. Think how that translates into the messages you, as leaders, are giving to the rest of your team. Think how it then gets amplified outside the business - in pitching; in marketing and PR; in recruitment; and in everyday word of mouth.

You need a pure signal if you are to be confident that you can amplify it without distortion, internally and externally. You need to 'find out who you are'...

To do that requires communication. Proper communication, listening as well as talking. It requires open-mindedness, not entrenched positions: if you really want to build a successful team you can't have people in it agreeing to disagree... See the Section 6 - on 'team' - for this point on steroids.

You also need to listen to what your customers want. What they *really* want, or would, if only they could have it. That means being clear about who your customers are, or more to the point, who you want to have as customers. See Section 7 for more on this...

You only have a sustainably successful, credible business when you have alignment across these three areas:

- your organisation or team's purpose
- what your customers really want from you, and what you can credibly and enthusiastically deliver that meets that need
- the products and services that connect these

Once you have that alignment, you're well on the way to having an organisation that you can pitch confidently, knowing that it stands up to scrutiny.

It also works as a benchmark for every decision you then make, allowing you to avoid the Siren Calls - attractive opportunities that are going to leave you on the rocks because they are not what you're good at or what your customers actually want.

Importantly, this pure signal only really works when the team is actively involved in both the development and the implementation of this. If it is unilaterally imposed on the team, there is no depth of understanding what it really means and therefore how to make it come alive. It can be seen as removed from real life.

And when it works, it can be the most invigorating bond, bringing a team together with a shared purpose and ambition. It creates a buzz.

Well, do you?

Early 'branding'…originally an anti-theft device…

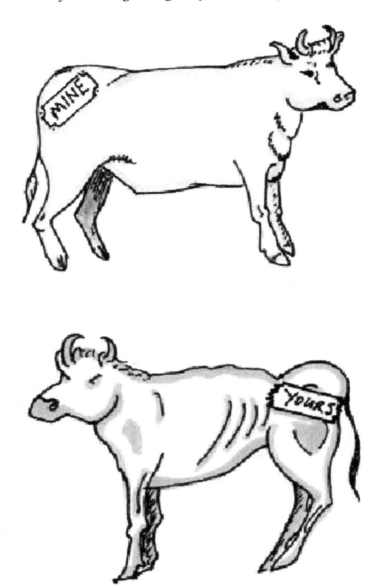

4 :

HOW INTEGRAL IS OUR BRANDING?

What we're really talking about here is 'brand', but not as people usually think about it. When people talk about 'brand' they usually mean the 'branding' or the marketing that is born out of brand: the things that you think you can leave to the Marketing department and wind them up for.

It's helpful to consider how the word 'brand' originally came into use, in the wild west where cowboys used a piece of red-hot metal to burn a 'brand' onto their cattle – a symbol that identified their cattle. It was an early anti-theft device.

At market, buyers came to recognise these symbols as signifiers of good (and bad) husbandry. Brand 'Mine' was used by a cowboy who looked after his cattle and would honour his word at market. Brand 'Yours' was used by a cowboy as we now use the word – someone had no respect for you or the animals, and although his prices might have been lower it was not necessarily a bargain. You paid your money and took your choice, guided by your accumulated knowledge about the men behind the marks.

Nothing has changed: your brand is your reputation, and that comes from every interaction anyone has with you and your organisation.

The brand is the sum of the parts. In professional services firms, many people think they are nothing to do with the brand, but in fact, *they* are intrinsically the brand. Clients are making their judgements not on how good any marketing material is, but on how good the experience is – the work, the service, the efficiency, the value for money. How far they trust *the people* to deliver on their promise.

The same is ultimately true in all businesses. Everything a customer sees has originated in the minds of individuals somewhere within the organisation. If they don't have a clear Purpose, they will be amplifying mixed messages.

The most exposing example of this is when the marketing team are presenting the company or it's products as one thing and HR are recruiting and training people according to a different Purpose. You create high expectations of the business that do not tally with customer experiences – a classic expectation gap.

I learned this most clearly early in my career when involved in the launch of a major new newspaper, the Sunday Correspondent. If you have never heard of it, it's not surprising: it only lasted a few months as the paper the CEO thought we were launching turned out to be very different from the one the Editor was actually masterminding. Church and State...

This rather serious disconnect only became clear four weeks before launch when the first dummy issues were printed, by when it was too late to change the marketing campaign. Purchasers drawn to the promise of a refreshing new paper as advertised were disappointed by the reality. It is not that it was a bad paper at all: it wasn't. It just wasn't the paper that buyers were expecting and it failed, fast.

This is by no means the only example I've seen though, many of them much more recently. When organisations don't have a clear purpose, people either make one up (leaving it to luck whether it matches the one their colleagues are working to) or they amplify nothing at all for fear of it being wrong. Neither course builds an inspiring brand.

So you can't devolve responsibility for your brand to the marketing department: it needs to embrace and be embraced by everyone if it is to be sustainable and effective.

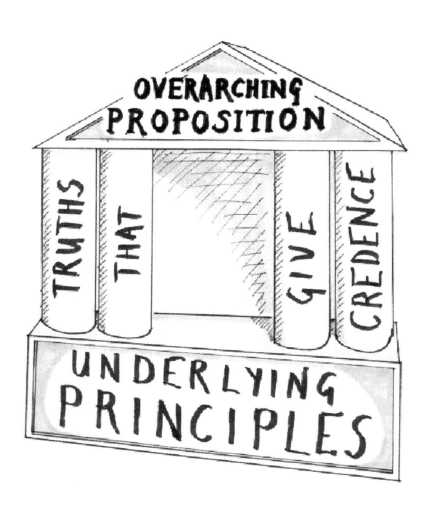

The brand house: built on solid foundations

5:
DOES IT ALL
ADD UP?

This is the most basic chart of all: I learned it in my first marketing agency job and I imagine every reader will have seen it at some point in their career.

It still works and I use it because it's splendidly simple: but the contents take hard work to get right.

The top is the over-arching proposition: what you, the team in charge, want everyone to know about you and your organisation, whoever they are – colleagues, customers, commentators, competition. It's not necessarily written for publication or for use in a presentation, it's more of an organising ambition than a slogan. The latter is generally best left to copywriters: the former must come from the team itself, even if facilitated along the way – otherwise, if it is imposed from afar, it means little and will have little effect.

It's surprising how much time and effort is involved in getting it right: it often gets down to semantics, but it's critically important as it is effectively that clear signal at the very heart of everything you are then going to amplify. Get that right and you know you can rely on it inspiring everyone and everything to work cohesively. Get it wrong and you have built in distortion from the outset.

That over-arching proposition is held up by pillars of truth: usually three or four. More than five and it's all getting too complicated: less than three and it's feeling a bit unstable.

Each of these is something that demonstrates that the overarching proposition is credible, not a wild dream.

It's helpful to think of these pillars as being like books on a shelf: you can see all the titles and glean what they mean, but different people will want to pick different books up to get into specific details.

At the bottom are the foundations. Everything is built on the way the organisation does business: your way of working and what matters to you. Sometimes, this is one line like 'to do everything for the best long-term outcome' which can be surprisingly helpful (see 'I'd have made it shorter if I'd had more time'...). More usually it is a summary of values or ethics. However you approach it, the important thing is that you mean it, and are prepared to live by it.

If these are behaviours you say you value, you need to show that you really value them. 'A principle is not a principle until it costs you money'. Make them part of your appraisal process so that people who live by them are demonstrably recognised. Many — perhaps most - companies, faced with making more money, are tempted to turn a blind eye to their values all too easily. Even well-respected global brands like VW (with Dieselgate) will sometimes let themselves stray, with well-chronicled disastrous results. 'It takes a lifetime to build a reputation and a second to destroy one.'

Goldman Sachs became a supremely successful organisation with the mantra 'Long-term greedy for our clients and for ourselves' underpinning everything. It's splendidly bold and when you think about it, it works (at least in the Goldman's world) because of the words 'long-term'. Those words mean you couldn't go for short-term profit: and that you had to put clients' success first because without that there would be no long-term. The blip that Goldmans suffered in the 2000s was when they lost their nerve in the frenzy of the boom and allowed people to chase short-term profits.

In this section more than any other section, the maxim 'I'd have made it shorter if I'd had more time' is important to remember. The Brand House relies on being distilled right down, and on the team genuinely engaging in it, not agreeing to disagree. It might feel tedious refining words and defining meanings, but you'll be glad you did. For a pitch, this is almost all you need as a structure. For a team or an organisation as a whole, it serves as a benchmark against which to evaluate future opportunities and ideas, working out which are Siren Calls and which are core strategic advances...

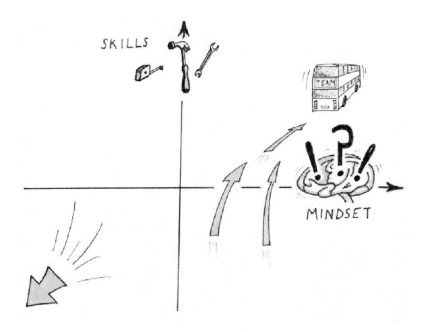

You can't teach mindset…

6:

DO WE REALLY
HAVE A TEAM?

You'll need the A-Team to make this happen if you're serious and ambitious. Everyone outside 'the workplace' understands this: in businesses and charities it is harder, partly because of employment law and partly because of corporate inertia. I've often been envious of how easy it is for the manager of a sports team to pick and choose the best players, putting those that don't fit the strategy onto the bench or even the transfer market. In corporate situations we have to work harder to build the right team with the right spirit.

Another favourite writer of mine, Jim Collins, talks about getting people on the bus. It's a good analogy, and his view is that you need to do this before you develop the strategy. In reality, it's a bit of both: you need good people to develop a good strategy, but you also need a good strategy to inform what people you actually need, and to attract them to join you. If you are reading this book you are probably de facto some way down the road on this.

Very often, the good people are sitting there already, but without the clarity and motivation to show what they can do. It doesn't take much discussion with bright people across a business to find there are plenty of them wishing they could do more but being held back by cautious or scared managers, or a culture that stifles initiative.

Our ad agency was built of people like that, people who 'didn't fit' their previous job but turned out to be hugely talented: they just needed an environment in which they could be themselves. It was something of a Magnificent Seven, a group of misfits drawn together by a common and exciting purpose, which is a very motivating force.

This simple quadrant is the essence of building your team. Attitude is more important than skills. Someone who technically has terrific skills but a bad attitude is a dangerous person to have on the team: they carry a lot of weight because they make a lot of money (usually) and a lot of noise (always) but they undermine the team ethic by behaving as gorillas, de-motivating the people around them and destroying team spirit.

Ideally you want people in the top right box. If people in the top left, and bottom right boxes have the capability of getting onto the bus then invest heavily in their development and help them onto the bus. If not, find a way to move them out of the business altogether. And the people in the bottom left box…they are in the wrong job. It will be better for them, and for you, if they move. Most of us have found ourselves in the wrong place at times: it has always been right to move on, even if it seems impossibly hard at the time. Sometimes we've needed some honesty to help us move on.

Find the right customers
and they will help find others for you

7:
DO WE TARGET THE RIGHT CUSTOMERS?

Now you have a clear purpose, and a talented, balanced, and motivated team to deliver it.

You need customers. The right customers. People who will be inspired by your organisation for what it is.

The quadrant in Section 6 can also be applied to targeting customers, with 'Potential Income' as the 'x' axis and 'Suitability' as the 'y' axis. The principle is the same: customers that don't fit are better served by another business, freeing you up to work with the ones that you are better equipped to service.

But this section is about Business Development.

At the top, you have the universe of people that could potentially buy from you but don't yet know what need of theirs you could answer.

Clearly, you need them to know about you so you need to get your message in front of them. Don't be afraid to be polarising in your message: you only want customers who actively like what you offer. It's a waste of time and money to pursue customers who are better suited to another product or service.

Once these ones are aware of you they become prospective customers or clients. You need to engage with them, edging them into the funnel itself where they are on your 'Customer Relationship Programme' (which hopefully will have a better name than that...).

This is likely to involve a courtship, whether personal or digital: preferably the former. There is no substitute for personal contact, but I understand that in fmcg for example it is rarely possible to have a proper personal relationship with any but the very best customers. Not so in Professional Services, however, even though a lot of 'sales'* people would like it to be so.

Throughout this process you are pitching you and your business. The more you can be showing of yourself – what you stand for, what you believe in, what makes you the most trustworthy, reliable and perhaps entertaining choice to work with – the more likely you are to get, and keep, the business. The next section explores a big part of how best to do this.

Once the prospective client becomes an actual client, they in turn become ambassadors, perhaps the most important part of all your 'marketing'. If you are doing your job well, they come to you for more work, saving you a huge amount of effort finding new clients…and they recommend you to other potential clients, with the same effect. A recommendation is clearly a big head-start in the next courtship process.

*NB Most people in Professional Services do not think they are in either 'Sales' or 'Marketing'. They are. In most cases, they are the only people who directly generate sales and the only people on whom the reputation of the business really rests.

Mind-blowing stuff…

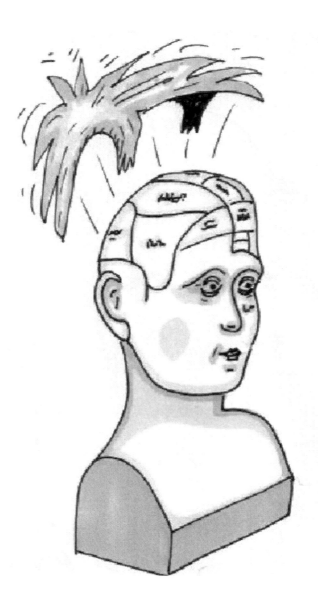

8:
WHAT'S ON
THEIR MINDS?

In the 19th century scientists first recognised that different
emotions and actions were dealt with by different parts of
the brain, and attempted to map that on those wonderful old
'Phrenology' busts. The details are not important here – my
purpose in using this engaging model is to make the point that
we need to think what is going on it other people's minds. To
walk in their shoes, to mix my metaphors.

It's amazing how many people, and businesses, think more
about themselves than they do about the people they're com-
municating with – and yet, without customers there is no
long-term business or job.

If you think back to the Venn Diagram discussed in Section
3, one of the main circles is 'clients'. Understanding them is
critical.

In our agency we realised that people were broadly 'left-brain
or 'right-brain' thinkers. Left-brain thinkers tend to prioritise

logic, discipline and organisation. Right-brain thinkers are drawn more to creativity, thinking in different patterns and reaching different conclusions. The advertising world is dominated by right-brain thinkers – creativity is their raison d'etre. But we realised that a good idea is only a successful idea if it is delivered efficiently and effectively, by a complementary team of left-brain thinkers.

The problem is that until then, creative people had looked down on 'process' people, and 'process' people had little regard for the ill-disciplined creative types. To have a durably successful business we needed both and we needed them both to be valued by each other, which became the case once people understood that they relied on each other. So - understanding what is going on in people's minds is important within your organisation.

When it comes to pitching, this understanding of 'the other person' is crucial too. Seeing ourselves as they see us. Meeting their needs. Pressing their hot buttons. All the clichés are founded in truth – it's not about what you know, it's about finding out what they want from you and tailoring it accordingly.

It's tempting when doing this just to think of the (many) business issues that will be on their mind. To get their full attention, though, you will have to get a sense of what makes them tick as human beings.

When it comes to pitching, there are three emotions in your audience's minds that you need to address. People often shuffle uncomfortably when I talk about this. Emotion and business are seen by many as mutually exclusive – yet, sometimes even unconsciously, emotion drives most of us in everything we do.

The first emotion is **Desire**. You need them to *want* to work with you, whether you're pitching yourself for a job, for investment in a start-up, for a major new contract or to inspire your team around a new vision.

What makes you the best option and how can you express this in a way that they can relate to? To know this, you need to find out about them.

But however much they *want* to work with you, you still have to overcome their **Fear**.

Even as a seasoned professional, it's still frightening to take on a new supplier, or recruit, or to invest in a company, however exciting they might seem: as the decision-maker you are very visible, and vulnerable to the 'if it ain't broke' contingent who would rather stick with what they know.

Your job in pitching to them is to give them enough *reassurance* to address those fears.

The third emotion is the gateway to all this – **Empathy**. Showing that you *understand* them; showing enough of the real you for them to get to know who you really are; and consequently building warmth and trust.

Anyone can practice a smooth pitch: what your prospect is looking for how you'll be further down the road, around the corner where there is no chance to practice.

Remember, the difference between winning and losing can often be the tiniest of margins. You need to stand out, and to do so you need to understand how you come across to other people. You need to recognise how much of communication is non-verbal, to do with your mannerisms and how you behave – and how you are outside of the 'set-piece' part of a presentation.

This is true for all forms of communication.

A great presentation: what lies beneath…

9:
ARE WE OVER-THINKING THIS?

And so we get to the point where you can build a really strong pitch. Remember here I am talking not only about the classic 'pitch' to win a major contract – I'm thinking of how you set out your stall to your team...or how you attract the very best people to your team...or how you convince hardened investors to back your growth plans.

Whatever your needs, the approach is very similar – and 'presentation skills' is only the icing on the cake, the peak of the mountain. However good your presentation skills are, you will be hard pushed to convince anyone if you haven't got a clear and compelling proposition.

Happily, your **presentation** skills will automatically become dramatically better if you do have that: a strong proposition means you talk with confidence...you look like you mean it: you don't have to bluff it.

The way you get there is, I'm afraid, through more hard work. Much of this **preparation** will have been done if you have read the preceding chapters and can honestly say that you have everything in place...and if not, I can safely say that your pitches will get markedly better if you work methodically through and get to the point where you can confidently make that claim.

Whatever, the preparation for a pitch of any sort falls broadly into two parts: firstly working out what your audience wants and needs from you, and then working out what you have got that they really want and need. It's the stuff in that intersection that matters – that is, in essence, your **proposition**. Part of the skill is editing out everything else so that all you have is a pure signal that won't distort when it is amplified.

The acid test is to think about your audience and what they will tell other people about your 'pitch'. Two observations on that:

-   sugar lumps. It may be apocryphal but I'm told that Maurice Saatchi, in the early days of his career, would sometimes be challenged by clients to add in more of their product benefits to the ad concept he had presented. He would calmly reach into the inevitable (in those days) bowl of sugar lumps on the board-room table and throw a handful towards the client saying simply 'catch'. When, as they inevitably would, they dropped the lot, he would send a single lump in their direction and they would – of course – catch it.

In the same way, we only catch one message at a time. You have to distil what you want to say right down, so that people can relay the basic message to other people.

People ask not so much *'what did they say'* as *'what were they like'* after a pitch, or an interview. If you really know what you are talking about and are confident in that message it will radiate: you will inspire and excite people with your manner. People will want to work with you.

So…No! You are not over-thinking this.

'To look this relaxed takes a lot of hard work' - Des Lynam

THE PURE SIGNAL

10:
HOW CLEAR IS
OUR MESSAGE?

This is perhaps the most important section in this little treatise. Is what you are saying clear enough, consistent enough, and motivating enough to be amplified with the confidence that it won't confuse?

If not, that is the root of unconfident pitching, of confusing communication within teams, in fact of many of the factors that prevent an organisation realising its potential.

When you have a pure signal, it can be amplified with virtuosity: the world can understand and join in. Think of the genius behind 'Who Dares Wins': no wonder people are proud to serve with the SAS. No wonder they are mythologised. No wonder their enemies know they have a serious challenge when the SAS is coming in. That line says it all. Amplify all you want.

I can vouch personally for a couple more examples, having been part of their creation, so I share them as references for what one might realistically be able to achieve.

In 2022, the Wales Men's team reached the finals of the World Cup for the first time since 1958: that's a gap of more than 60 years – although they did qualify for the finals of Euros in both 2016 and 2020, both landmarks in the renaissance of Welsh football.

That 2016 landmark was the first time a slogan 'Together Stronger' was adopted by Wales, and it is the title of a BBC series charting their renaissance.

'Together Stronger' is a much deeper message than it appears and is the direct development of the work I led with the Welsh Football Association when their current CEO first took the reins. His ambition, now realised in exemplary fashion, was to break what we described as the biannual cycle of hope and despair. Every two years, as the FAW approached the next qualifying stage of a major international tournament, there would be a huge swell of optimism: 'maybe this time'.

Each time there was nothing more to it than optimism. No serious depth of commitment behind the scenes to give it any substance...and so it inevitably ended in deep despair – and recriminations.

Breaking the cycle needed myths debunked (e.g., 'Wales is too much a rugby country to win at football'. Exhibit A: New Zealand had a much stronger record in international football...) but the biggest challenge was the difference between the attitude on the pitch and off it. The Council, the most senior part of FAW governance, expected the team to play like Brazil whilst they watched on, eating prawn sandwiches and drinking fine wine.

Never was this demotivating attitude clearer than when a new member of the squad, getting off the plane for his first away match, saw a distinctly out-of-shape fan with a flag draped over his naked torso, can of lager in his one hand whilst with the other, shaking each team member by the hand as they disembarked. When this new team member asked a famous, more experienced team-mate how this fan had managed to break through the cordon, the answer came back 'He's the Chairman.'

As we pondered how to break this malaise and get the whole of Welsh football to work together, my colleague Tim Lawler found that the motto emblazoned on every Welsh football shirt **Gorau Chwarae Cyd Chwarae** , ignored by everyone but there in plain sight, translates literally as 'The best play is team play'...

Intriguingly it had only been added in 1951, not long before Wales played in the 1958 World Cup finals.

We had the first cut of our pure signal and were able to use it to start bringing together the whole of Welsh football and to break that cycle of optimism and despair. Clever wordsmithing took it from an internal principle to being Together Stronger, a rallying cry that continues to power Welsh football years later.

Strangely, such simple solutions are rarely the result of a flash of inspiration (see *'I'd have made it shorter if I'd had more time'* in the Intro) but they can spring suddenly from a conducive process and enquiring minds, as was the case with Fortnum's as we were exploring how to reinvigorate this majestic British business in readiness for its fourth century. What had made it such a global icon was two periods in its history when it had been a powerhouse of both invention and rigorous delivery. Like a West End theatre, at its best Fortnum's gave its customers a stimulating, memorable creative experience, all built on reliable stage management.

We knew we needed to rekindle that spirit in the 21st Century Fortnum's and developed the overarching proposition 'A fountain of inspiration in food, drink, celebration and entertainment'. We wanted a mantra to encapsulate this and how we wanted everyone in the business to approach everything they did – from serving a customer to sourcing a new product. So we took the famous F & M and made it stand for Fabulous & Meticulous. Crucially this was both easy to communicate throughout the business and also easy to remember, whatever one was doing. It wasn't enough for a new product to be technically excellent – the whole experience across look, feel, taste, packaging, description, and the purchase experience - had to be memorable and exciting. Every time.

It meant everyone had to be using their left brain – delivery – and their right brain – creativity – all the time, and was used to inspire the reinvigoration of every facet of the business.

These examples, two of my favorites, illustrate that it's about far more than good presentation. It's about catching people's imagination, making them want to work with you because they'll enjoy it AND get results.

If you can't
communicate it, it
might as well not
exist.

THANK YOU

To you, for reading these musings. I hope that you have gleaned at least a few helpful thoughts on how to marshal your organisation to get your message across like a graceful swan.

To Leo Campbell, who brought out in me the latent radical and helped inspire our new and highly effective approach to pitching whilst we worked together at Claydon Heeley and beyond.

To Tim Lawler, who came up with the name of this book as well as being a fantastic part of developing the thinking throughout, and...

To Bina Tarulli who has brought her talented art direction to everything I do.

To the many clients I've worked with over the years for allowing or even encouraging me to challenge you in the pursuit of ever-better outcomes throughout your organisations. I've loved working with you...and I still do!

Specifically to George Roberts, UK CEO at Cushman & Wakefield, who suggested that I write a book around the charts I use in my work.

And to my wife Miranda who encouraged me to illustrate the book by sending me on a Diploma course in Cartooning...I perhaps should have waited until the course was finished before doing these cartoons!

Thank you all.

ABOUT
THE AUTHOR

Edward Mason coaches leaders in strategy and communication. This includes 'presentation skills' - often in conjunction with coaches from the theatre and TV world - but mostly it is about helping organisations identify the potency their organisation has and how then to communicate it in a way that differentiates them.

He has worked with leaders in a large number of start-ups to global players across many different sectors: there are testimonials from some of them below to give an idea of the diverse experience he brings.

He is married to a Psychodynamic Counsellor and is fascinated by the underpinning philosophy of helping people to take responsibility for their own destinies. The concept that you can't change the past but you can change your future applies as much to organisations as it does to individuals.

He comes across as quite conventional - which helps people feel comfortable in engagements - but that's emphatically not how his mind work. He believes that constant reinvigoration is an essential ingredient of long-term success, however much history and heritage you may have.

Printed in Great Britain
by Amazon

31624423R00040